Be a Good Friend!

by Jennifer Waters

Content and Reading Adviser: Mary Beth Fletcher, Ed.D.
Educational Consultant/Reading Specialist
The Carroll School, Lincoln, Massachusetts

Spyglass
BOOKS

COMPASS POINT BOOKS

Minneapolis, Minnesota

Compass Point Books
3722 West 50th Street, #115
Minneapolis, MN 55410

Visit Compass Point Books on the Internet at *www.compasspointbooks.com*
or e-mail your request to *custserv@compasspointbooks.com*

Photographs ©: Visuals Unlimited/Jim Whitmer, cover; Visuals Unlimited/D. Yeske, 5, 17;
Visuals Unlimited/Jeff Greenberg, 7, 9, 13; Visuals Unlimited/Cheyenne Rouse, 11;
Visuals Unlimited/Cheryl A. Ertelt, 15; Two Coyotes Studio/Mary Foley, 19, 20, 21.

Project Manager: Rebecca Weber McEwen
Editor: Heidi Schoof
Photo Selectors: Rebecca Weber McEwen and Heidi Schoof
Designer: Jaime Martens

Library of Congress Cataloging-in-Publication Data

Waters, Jennifer.
  Be a good friend! / by Jennifer Waters.
     p. cm. — (Spyglass books)
Summary: Enumerates the qualities that make someone a good friend.
Includes bibliographical references and index.
  ISBN 0-7565-0376-0
  1. Friendship in children—Juvenile literature. [1. Friendship.]
  I. Title. II. Series.
  BF723.F68 .W38 2002
  177'.62—dc21
                              2002002540

Contents

Good Friends

What makes a good friend? Good friends help each other. How should a person *behave* to be a good friend?

Caring

A good friend *cares* about you.
A good friend cares about
how you feel.
If you care about someone
you know, you can be
a good friend.

Listening

A good friend listens to you.
A nice way to show you
are listening to your friend
is to ask questions.
If you are a good listener,
you can be a good friend.

9

Sharing

A good friend shares.
Good friends share stories, toys, and treats.
If you are good at sharing, you can be a good friend.

11

Being Honest

A good friend is *honest.*
Good friends tell each other the *truth.*
If you are honest, you can be a good friend.

13

Showing Respect

A good friend **respects** you.
You can show your friends
respect by being careful of
their feelings.
If you are respectful,
you can be a good friend.

14

Being Helpful

A good friend is helpful.
Good friends are kind and
help each other.
If you are helpful, you can be
a good friend.

17

Being Brave

A good friend is *brave.*
A good friend will do
the right thing even if
it is scary.
If you are brave, you can be
a good friend.

19

Friendship Bracelet

You can make a friendship bracelet.

You will need:
- string
- scissors
- a ruler

1. Cut three pieces of string that are 8 inches long.

2. Hold the pieces together and tie a knot at one end.

3. Braid the three pieces together.

4. Tie a knot in the loose end.

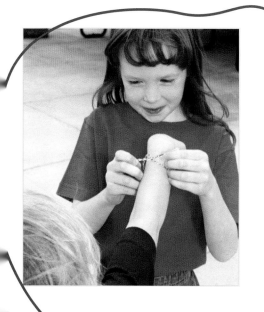

5. Tie the bracelet around your friend's wrist. Don't tie it too tight!

Glossary

behave–to act a certain way

brave–when people do or say things
even though they are scared to

care–to be interested in what another
person thinks and feels

honest–describes someone who tells
the truth

respect–to believe that how other
people feel is important

truth–what really happened, or how
a person really feels

Learn More

Books

Friendship Stories You Can Share.
New York: SeaStar Books, 2001.

Hood, Susan. *The New Kid.* Brookfield,
Conn.: The Millbrook Press, 1998.

Schwartz, Linda. *What Would You Do?*
Illustrated by Beverly Armstrong.
Santa Barbara, Calif.: The Learning
Works, 1990.

Web Sites

Kidshealth.org/kid/feeling/friend/
about_friends.html

myhero.com

Index

GR: F
Word Count: 203

From Jennifer Waters

I live near the Rocky Mountains,
but the ocean is my favorite place.
I like to write songs and books.
I hope you enjoyed this book.

24